_____

To

_____

From

_____

Date

Angels Among the Roses

Paintings by *Donald Zolan*

HARVEST HOUSE PUBLISHERS

EUGENE, OREGON

Angels Among the Roses

Published by Harvest House Publishers
Eugene, Oregon 97402
www.harvesthousepublishers.com

ISBN 978-0-7369-3872-3

Donald Zolan: For information regarding art prints by Donald Zolan, please contact:
The Zolan Company, LLC, Donaldz798@aol.com; www.zolan.com

Design and production by Garborg Design Works, Savage, Minnesota

Harvest House Publishers has made every effort to trace the ownership of all poems and quotes. In the event of a question arising from the use of a poem or quote, we regret any error made and will be pleased to make the necessary correction in future editions of this book.

Printed in China

11 12 13 14 15 16 17 18 19 / LP / 10 9 8 7 6 5 4 3 2 1

WHAT WILL I BE WHEN I GROW UP?

Answer in the Stillness

by Donald Zolan, Hershey, Pennsylvania

I climbed up onto the chair at the desk in Grandpa's bedroom and laid out my supplies: drawing paper, a nine-color paint set, two brushes, a tube of white paint, and a glass filled with water. I was four years old, and it was summer in my small Illinois hometown, but I wanted to paint before I went out to play. Mom and Dad had been excited about a drawing of a horse I had shown them the night before. I wanted to do something even better. I took the comic book from my pocket and smoothed it out on the desk. There was a picture of Donald Duck playing cymbals and a drum. I spent a couple of hours drawing and painting my favorite cartoon character just the way it appeared in the book. When I finished, I ran down the hall into the kitchen, where my mom was busy ironing clothes near the window, the white linen curtains undulating about her in the breeze.

She stared at my painting a long time, while I shuffled my feet impatiently. Finally, she looked at me.

"You did this all by yourself?" she asked.

I nodded and showed her the original.

She smiled. "This is wonderful, Donny! When your father gets home tonight, I'll talk to him about getting you some more art supplies."

Ecstatic, I went outside. Next to the garage was a patch of grass and dirt with a low granite boulder around which Mom had planted flowers. I had spent many afternoons on that rock, tracking ants or looking at the clouds. I sat on the sun-warmed surface, took a deep breath, and looked around me. The roses seemed to glitter in the light. Bees darted among the marigolds. I reached out to try catching a passing orange and blue butterfly and just missed it.

Then I peered closely at my paint-smudged palm. The breeze ruffled my hair the way my dad did. I thought of him going off in his big white truck each morning to deliver milk. *What will I be when I grow up?* I wondered.

For a moment the breeze stilled, and it was completely quiet. "You will be an artist," said a gentle voice just above my head. I looked up but saw no one. I looked back down at my hands. The voice continued, "A fine artist. And you will sign your name like this." In the dirt at my feet I found myself tracing a capital Z with a horizontal stroke across it, a capital *O* with a lowercase *l* through it, and a small *a* and *n* followed by a period. I sat staring at it. "An artist," the voice repeated.

The breeze picked up again and wafted gently over my face. I stood. Everything was the same as before—the sun, the bees, the blossoms—but it all looked clearer somehow, more vibrant.

I trotted into the house to find my mother. "Mommy," I said, tugging the hem of her dress, "there was a voice talking to me out there."

"Who was it?" she asked with a curious expression.

"I'm not sure," I said and explained the voice and what it told me.

She put down the iron and bent to hug me. "Always remember that voice, Donny," she whispered. "That was your guardian angel."

Soon after, my parents bought me an easel and more art supplies. I painted every day. At age 11, I earned a scholarship to The School of the Art Institute of Chicago and later to the American Academy of Art. Today I earn my living as an artist and still sign my name as I was instructed years ago. I have portrayed many different subjects. But most of all, I love to paint children to try capturing the image of that time of life when I believe we are most receptive to God's will, the time when I was fortunate enough to hear my true calling in an angel's gentle voice.

WHAT SUNSHINE IS TO
FLOWERS, SMILES ARE TO
HUMANITY. THESE ARE BUT
TRIFLES, TO BE SURE; BUT
SCATTERED ALONG LIFE'S
PATHWAY, THE GOOD THEY DO
IS INCONCEIVABLE.

JOSEPH ADDISON

Angels descending, bring from above,
Echoes of mercy, whispers of love.
FANNY J. CROSBY

There is not the least
flower but seems to hold
up its head, and to look
pleasantly, in the secret
sense of the goodness of
its heavenly Maker.

ROBERT SOUTH

Adopt the pace of nature: her secret is patience.
RALPH WALDO EMERSON

SWEET SOULS AROUND US WATCH US STILL,
PRESS NEARER TO OUR SIDE;
INTO OUR THOUGHTS, INTO OUR PRAYERS,
WITH GENTLE HELPINGS GLIDE.

HARRIET BEECHER STOWE

A good deed is never lost.
He who sows courtesy, reaps friendship;
he who plants kindness, gathers love;
pleasure bestowed upon a grateful mind
was never sterile, but generally
gratitude begets reward.

ST. BASIL

Hope is like the
wing of an angel,
soaring up to heaven,
and bearing our prayers
to the throne of God.

JEREMY TAYLOR

As dew to the blossom,
and bud to the bee,
as the scent to the rose,
are those memories to me.

AMELIA B. WELBY

LOVELY FLOWERS ARE TH[

All God's pleasures are simple ones;
the rapture of a May morning
sunshine, the stream blue and green,
kind words, benevolent acts,
the glow of good humor.

FREDERICK WILLIAM ROBERTSON

Happiness is like a butterfly
which, when pursued,
is always beyond our grasp,
but, if you will sit down quietly,
may alight upon you.

NATHANIEL HAWTHORNE

'Tis my faith that every flower

Enjoys the air it breathes.

WILLIAM WORDSWORTH

MILES OF GOD'S GOODNESS.

WILLIAM WILBERFORCE

HOPE IS THE
THING WITH FEATHERS
THAT PERCHES IN
THE SOUL,
AND SINGS THE TUNE—
WITHOUT THE WORDS.
AND NEVER STOPS
AT ALL.

EMILY DICKINSON

Nothing multiplies so much as kindness.

JOHN RAY

JUST LIVING IS NOT
ENOUGH... ONE
MUST HAVE SUNSHINE,
FREEDOM, AND A
LITTLE FLOWER.

HANS CHRISTIAN ANDERSEN

Far away there in the sunshine are my highest aspirations. I may not reach them but I can look up and see their beauty, believe in them, and try to follow where they lead.

LOUISA MAY ALCOTT

An angel can illuminate the thought and mind of man by strengthening the power of vision.

ST. THOMAS AQUINAS

*It is heaven upon earth
to have a man's mind
move in charity, rest in
providence, and turn
upon the poles of truth.*

FRANCIS BACON

GRATITUDE
IS A SOIL
ON WHICH
JOY
THRIVES.

BERTHOLD AUERBACH

*Walk boldly and wisely
in that light thou hast—
There is a hand above
will help thee on.*

PHILIP JAMES BAILEY

To be glad of life because it gives you the chance to love and to work and to play and to look up at the stars; to be satisfied with your possessions but not contented with yourself until you have made the best of them. . .and to spend as much time as you can, with body and with spirit, in God's out-of-doors, these are little guideposts on the footpath to peace.

HENRY VAN DYKE

THOSE WHO BRING SUNSHINE TO THE LIVES OF OTHERS CANNOT KEEP IT FROM THEMSELVES.

JAMES M. BARRIE

Gratitude is a nice touch of beauty added last of all to the countenance, giving a classic beauty, an angelic loveliness, to the character.

THEODORE PARKER

Flowers are love's truest language.

PARK BENJAMIN

Every charitable act is a stepping stone toward heaven.

HENRY WARD
BEECHER

18

Nothing but heaven itself is better than a friend who is really a friend.

PLAUTUS

WHATEVER IS TO REACH THE HEART MUST COME FROM ABOVE.

LUDWIG VAN BEETHOVEN

Rose is a rose is a rose is a rose.

GERTRUDE STEIN

19

CUT A PATH INTO THE
HEAVEN OF GLORY,
LEAVING A TRACK OF LIGHT
FOR MEN TO WONDER AT.

WILLIAM BLAKE

*Every moment is a
golden one for him
who has the vision to
recognize it as such.*

HENRY MILLER

Happiness is a glory
shining far down upon us
from heaven. She is a divine
dew, which the soul feels
dropping upon it from
the amaranth bloom and
golden fruitage of paradise.

CHARLOTTE BRONTE

*Hope springs eternal
in the human breast.*

ALEXANDER POPE

The fairest flower in
the garden of creation
is a young mind,
offering and unfolding
itself to the influence
of divine wisdom, as
the heliotrope turns its
sweet blossoms to the sun.

JAMES EDWARD SMITH

Loveliest of love things are they
On earth that soonest pass away.
The rose that lives its little hour
Is prized beyond
The sculptured flower.

WILLIAM CULLEN BRYANT

Earth laughs in flowers.

RALPH WALDO EMERSON

Nature is the art of God.

THOMAS BROWNE

I CANNOT
BE CONTENT
WITH LESS
THAN HEAVEN.

PHILIP JAMES BAILEY

Heaven lies about us in our infancy.

WILLIAM WORDSWORTH

Sing out my soul, thy songs of joy;
Such as a happy bird will sing,
Beneath a Rainbow's lovely arch,
In early spring.

WILLIAM HENRY DAVIES

THE HOPE OF HEAVEN UNDER TROUBLE

LIKE WIND AND SAILS TO THE SOUL.

MUSIC IS WELL SAID TO B

When you have once seen the glow of happiness on the face of a beloved person, you know that a man can have no vocation but to awaken that light on the faces surrounding him; and you are torn by the thought of the unhappiness and night you cast, by the mere fact of living, in the hearts you encounter.

ALBERT CAMUS

LITTLE DEEDS OF KINDNESS,
LITTLE WORDS OF LOVE,
HELP TO MAKE EARTH HAPPY
LIKE THE HEAVEN ABOVE.

JULIA FLETCHER CARNEY, "LITTLE THINGS"

The rainbow which hangs a splendid circle in the heights of heaven, is also formed by the same sun in the dew-drop of the lowly flower.

JEAN PAUL RICHTER

HE SPEECH OF ANGELS.

THOMAS CARLYLE

27

*A single
grateful thought
toward heaven
is the most
perfect prayer.*

GOTTHOLD EPHRAIM LESSING

Silently, one by one,
in the infinite meadows of heaven,
Blossomed the lovely stars,
the forget-me-nots of the angels.

HENRY WADSWORTH LONGFELLOW

*The grand essentials of happiness are:
something to do, something to love, and something to hope for.*

ALLAN K. CHALMERS

Kindness is the
sunshine in which
virtue grows.

ROBERT INGERSOLL

Happiness is no vague dream, of that I now feel certain.

GEORGE SAND

Flowers have spoken to me more than I can tell in written words. They are the hieroglyphics of angels, loved by all men for the beauty of the character, though few can decipher even fragments of their meaning.

LYDIA M. CHILD

TO SEE A WORLD IN A GRAIN OF SAND, AND A HEAVEN IN A WILD FLOWER, HOLD INFINITY IN THE PALM OF YOUR HAND, AND ETERNITY IN AN HOUR.

WILLIAM BLAKE

The flowers are nature's jewels, with whose wealth she decks her summer beauty.

GEORGE CROLY

Happiness is like manna; it is to be gathered in grains, and enjoyed every day. It will not keep; it cannot be accumulated; nor have we got to go out of ourselves or into remote places to gather it, since it has rained down from a Heaven, at our very door.

TRYON EDWARDS

32

The song of heaven is ever new; for daily thus and nightly, new discoveries are made of God's unbounded wisdom, power, and love, which give the understanding larger room, and swell the hymn with ever-growing praise.

ROBERT POLLOK

HAVE YOU HAD A KINDNESS SHOWN?

PASS IT ON;

'TWAS NOT GIVEN FOR THEE ALONE,

PASS IT ON;

LET IT TRAVEL DOWN THE YEARS,

LET IT WIPE ANOTHER'S TEARS,

'TIL IN HEAVEN THE DEED APPEARS—

PASS IT ON.

HENRY BURTON

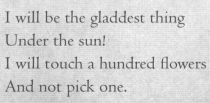

I will be the gladdest thing
Under the sun!
I will touch a hundred flowers
And not pick one.

EDNA ST. VINCENT MILLAY

To reach the
port of heaven,
we must sail
sometimes with
the wind,
and sometimes
against it, but
we sail, and
not drift, nor
lie at anchor.

OLIVER WENDELL HOLMES

BUT LET ALL WHO TAKE REFUGE IN YOU BE GLAD;

LET THEM EVER SING FOR JOY.

SPREAD YOUR PROTECTION OVER THEM,

THAT THOSE WHO LOVE YOUR NAME MAY REJOICE IN YOU.

THE BOOK OF PSALMS

If the only prayer you said in
your whole life was, "thank
you," that would suffice.
MEISTER ECKHART

*Happiness
resides not in
possessions
and not in gold;
the feeling of
happiness dwells
in the soul.*
DEMOCRITUS

*E*very saint in heaven is as a flower in
the garden of God, and holy love is the
fragrance and sweet odor that they all send
forth, and with which they fill the bowers
of that paradise above.

JONATHAN EDWARDS

O, beautiful rainbow, all woven of light!

There's not in thy tissue one shadow of night.

Heaven surely is open when thou dost appear.

And, bending above thee, the angels draw near,

And sing—"The rainbow! the rainbow! The smile of God is here!"

MRS. SARAH JOSEPHA HALE

IF I HAVE FREEDOM IN MY LOVE,
AND IN MY SOUL AM FREE,
ANGELS ALONE THAT SOAR ABOVE,
ENJOY SUCH LIBERTY.

RICHARD LOVELACE

Heaven, the treasury
of everlasting joy.

WILLIAM SHAKESPEARE

Earth has no sorrow that heaven cannot heal.

THOMAS MOORE

WHAT IS SO RARE AS A DAY IN JUNE?
THEN, IF EVER, COME PERFECT DAYS;
THEN HEAVEN TRIES EARTH IF IT BE IN TUNE,
AND OVER IT SOFTLY HER WARM EAR LAYS.

JAMES RUSSELL LOWELL, "A DAY IN JUNE"

*Flowers... are a proud
assertion that a ray of
beauty outvalues all the
utilities of the world.*

RALPH WALDO EMERSON

Hope is the dream of a soul awake.

FRENCH PROVERB

I believe that if one always looked at the sky, one would end up with wings.

GUSTAVE FLAUBERT

Heaven is the day of which grace is the dawn; the rich, ripe fruit of which grace is the lovely flower; the inner shrine of that most glorious temple to which grace forms the approach and outer court.

Thomas Guthrie

O, my Luve's like a red, red rose,
That's newly sprung in June.
O, my Luve's like the melodie,
That's sweetly play'd in tune.

Robert Burns, "A Red, Red Rose"

Home is the sphere of harmony and peace,
the spot where angels find a resting place,
when bearing blessings, they descend to earth.

Mrs. Sarah Josepha Hale

THE LOVE OF HEAVEN
MAKES ONE HEAVENLY.

WILLIAM SHAKESPEARE

*Heaven's the perfection
of all that can be said or
thought—riches, delight,
harmony, health, beauty;
and all these not subject
to the waste of time, but
in their height eternal.*

JAMES SHIRLEY

The Amen! of Nature
is always a flower.

OLIVER WENDELL HOLMES

O welcome,
pure-eyed Faith,
white-handed Hope,
Thou hovering angel,
girt with golden wings!

JOHN MILTON

Hope is the word which God has written on the brow of every man.

VICTOR HUGO

Write your name in kindness, love, and mercy on the hearts of thousands you come in contact with year by year, and you will never be forgotten. Your name and your good deeds will shine as the stars of heaven.

THOMAS CHALMERS

The natural flights of the human mind are not from pleasure to pleasure but from hope to hope.

SAMUEL JOHNSON

THE GENEROUS WHO IS ALWAYS JUST, AND THE JUST WHO IS ALWAYS GENEROUS, MAY, UNANNOUNCED, APPROACH THE THRONE OF HEAVEN.

J.C. LAVATER

I try to
avoid looking
forward or
backward,
and try to keep
looking upward.

CHARLOTTE BRONTE

I LOVE TO
THINK OF NATURE
AS AN UNLIMITED
BROADCASTING STATION,
THROUGH WHICH GOD
SPEAKS TO US EVERY
HOUR, IF WE WILL
ONLY TUNE IN.

GEORGE WASHINGTON CARVER

*Let us not
be justices of
the peace, but
angels of peace.*

ST. THERESA OF LISIEUX

*Kind hearts are the gardens
Kind thoughts are the roots,
Kind words are the flowers,
Kind deeds are the fruits.*

*Take care of your garden,
And keep out the weeds.
Fill it with sunshine,
Kind words and kind deeds.*

HENRY WADSWORTH LONGFELLOW

HEAVEN WILL BE THE ENDLESS PORTION OF EVERY
MAN WHO HAS HEAVEN IN HIS SOUL.

HENRY WARD BEECHER

If instead of a gem, or even a flower, we should cast the gift of a loving thought
into the heart of a friend, that would be giving as the angels give.

GEORGE MacDONALD